YOUR KNOWLEDGE HAS VALUE

Lea Lorena Jerns

"Incidents in the life of a Slave Girl" by Harriet Jacobs

An Essay

GRIN Verlag

Bibliografische Information der Deutschen Nationalbibliothek:

Die Deutsche Bibliothek verzeichnet diese Publikation in der Deutschen National-
bibliografie; detaillierte bibliografische Daten sind im Internet über http://dnb.d-
nb.de/ abrufbar.

Imprint:

Copyright © 2013 GRIN Verlag GmbH
Druck und Bindung: Books on Demand GmbH, Norderstedt Germany
ISBN: 978-3-656-66989-0

This book at GRIN:

http://www.grin.com/en/e-book/274165/incidents-in-the-life-of-a-slave-girl-by-har-
riet-jacobs

GRIN - Your knowledge has value

Der GRIN Verlag publiziert seit 1998 wissenschaftliche Arbeiten von Studenten, Hochschullehrern und anderen Akademikern als eBook und gedrucktes Buch. Die Verlagswebsite www.grin.com ist die ideale Plattform zur Veröffentlichung von Hausarbeiten, Abschlussarbeiten, wissenschaftlichen Aufsätzen, Dissertationen und Fachbüchern.

Visit us on the internet:

http://www.grin.com/

http://www.facebook.com/grincom

http://www.twitter.com/grin_com

Humboldt-Universität zu Berlin

Institut für Anglistik & Amerikanistik

Seminar: American Literary History I: From the Beginnings to World War I

November 17, 2012

Lea Lorena Jerns

Essay

Harriet Jacobs, *Incidents in the Life of a Slave Girl*

Harriet Jacobs, "Incidents in the Life of a Slave Girl"

Harriet Jacobs as a courageous brave strong-willed girl/woman

Harriet Jacobs "Incidents in the life of a slave girl" was published in 1861. Harriet Jacobs tells us her story from her perspective as somebody born as a slave. "The pseudonymous narrator, Linda Brent, is caught between the brutal, exploitative bonds of slavery and the idealized, altruistic bonds of true womanhood." (Sherman, 167). Harriet Jacobs was "the first American woman known to have authored a slave narrative in the United States [...]." (Jacobs, 804). Through Harriet Jacob's story one can gain a deep insight into the hard life and into the soul and feelings of Harriet Jacobs as Linda Brent. One can learn a lot about courage, bravery, willpower and determination – briefly speaking: about a strong girl/woman who never gave up.

She didn't realize before the age of six that she was a slave. Her life was filled with love from those who surrounded her. There were her mother, her younger brother, who was "a bright, affectionate child" (Jacobs, 805) as well as her maternal grandmother who was like a treasure to her (Jacobs, 805). When Linda's mother died she left her and her younger brother William to the care of her mistress, whom Linda loved like her own mother. At the age of twelve her mistress passed away and Linda became "property" of the mistress's sister's daughter. Mr. Flint became her new master as the mistress's sister's daughter was only 5 years old. At this point her so far more or less "happy days" ended. That will bring me to my thesis, because from this point on Linda had to be a powerful, strong girl as she had to go through the mistreating by Mr. Flint. When Linda for instance tells her master about her wish to get married to her black lover, he humiliates her by saying: "Well, I'll soon convince you whether I am your master, or the nigger fellow you honor so highly. [...] He sprang upon [her] like a tiger, and gave [her] a stunning blow." (Jacobs, 809). He continued threatening her by pointing out: "Do you know that I have a right to do as I like with you, - that I can kill you, if I please?" (Jacobs, 810). But Linda nonetheless keeps her courage and remains faithful to herself - even if she might therefore put herself in grave danger: "You have struck me for answering you honestly. How I despise you!" (Jacobs, 809).

Later on Harriet Jacobs had to go through another hard period in her life. When she hid from her master, Mr. Flint, in the attic of a small shed next to her grandmother's house, "[…] which was no more than a few hundred yards from her master's plantation" (Starr Alonzo, 118), for seven years, she had to live under very harsh conditions: "[…] the slope was so sudden that I could not turn on the other [side] without hitting the roof. The rats and mice ran over my bed […]. I suffered for air even more than for light. […] [F]or weeks I was tormented by hundreds of little red insects […]. " (Jacobs, 818 - 819). Due to this detailed description the reader can imagine her uncomfortable situation very well and would possibly assume that she couldn't handle such a situation for a long time – but Harriet Jacobs again behaved in such a brave and strong-willed way. She always kept her goal in mind to achieve freedom and happiness for her and her children one day. Watching her children through a little hole as well as her caring grandmother gave her confidence.

After those seven years she was able to travel to the North, where she stayed at Mrs. Bruce's house. She finally felt save there, but it wasn't meant to be. Although Mr. Flint had already died in the meantime, Harriet Jacobs was again in danger of being caught - by Mr. Flint's daughter and her husband this time: "Reader, if you have never been a slave, you cannot imagine the acute sensation of suffering at my heart, when I read the names of Mr. and Mrs. Dodge (Dodge is the married name of Emily Flint, Brent's legal owner.) […]." (Jacobs, 821). So, she had to flee and hide once more. Again Harriet Jacobs as Linda Brent didn't waste a single thought on giving up or being hopeless. She was sure that she would be a free person at some point and wouldn't have to live in fear or hide from anyone. She did what had to be done:

"A carriage was hastily ordered; and, closely veiled, I followed Mrs. Bruce, taking the baby again with me into exile." (Jacobs, 821).

In the end Harriet Jacobs reached her goal for which she fought so tenaciously: "Reader, my story ends with freedom [...]. I and my children are now free!" (Jacobs, 825). She had many struggles in her life. She went through the mistreatment of Mr. Flint, she got through the seven years where she lived in a kind of hole and didn't abandon hope, even when she thought she would finally be safe, but shortly after had to realize that she was wrong. *"Incidents in the Life of a Slave Girl"* is therefore not just a sad story of a slave's life but an admirable slave narrative of a girl/woman who never let anybody get her down.

Works cited

Jacobs, Harriet. "Incidents in the Life of a Slave Girl." *The Norton Anthology of American Literature, Shorter Edition (7th ed.).* Ed. Nina Baym. New York: W. W. Norton & Company, 2008. 804 – 825. Print.

Sherman, Sarah Way. "Moral Experience in Harriet Jacob's Incidents in the Life of a Slave Girl." *NWSA Journal 2, 2,* (1990):. 167 – 185. Print.

Starr Alonzo, Andrea. "A Study of Two Women's Slave Narratives: 'Incidents in The Life of a Slave Girl' and 'The History of Mary Prince'." *Women's Studies Quarterly 17, 3/4,* (1989):. 118 – 122. Print.